THE DREAM POWER JOURNAL

A System for Organizing Your Dreams to Enhance Your Life

Cynthia Richmond

Published by
DreamPower Publishing™
Sedona, Arizona

DreamPower Publishing™
Sedona, Arizona

Copyright ©2010 by Cynthia Richmond
All Rights reserved,
including the right of reproduction
in whole or in part in any form.

First DreamPower™ Edition

DreamPower Publishing™
is a registered trademark.

Designed by Rocky Berlier
Manufactured in the United States of America

ISBN 9-781-453-832387

Dedication

I dedicate this book to every person who has ever shared a dream with me. Especially, my long time dream groups in Los Angeles and Sedona, your trust allowed me to do the research needed to be of service in the sacred world of dreams.
Thank you.

Acknowledgements

I'd like to express my sincere gratitude to my amazing husband, sculptor, John M. Soderberg, PhD, for his unwavering love, support and eagle-eye editing. Thank you my darling. To my long-time friend, Rocky Berlier, who designed this cover, and used his incredible skills both artistic and technical to create this volume in the form you see it, you are a rock star. To every television program, radio show and print media editor or producer who gave me a chance to help their viewers, listeners and readers to benefit from the gift of their nightly dreams. To every author and researcher in the world of dreams who has shared their savvy, research and experience for the benefit of us all. Thank you for your generosity. And finally, to Suzanne, Heather and Misty with love, you are the bright lights in my life.

Preface

I have had the good fortune to meet many of our nation's dream experts and a sprinkling from other countries as well. Some bring immense academic acumen to the dream worktable, others a sacred spiritual approach and some the scientific method through the disciplines of psychiatry and psychology. All are integral in our understanding of the organic gift our dreams bring each day. They are indeed a beautiful tool moving us toward self-realization, if we will only pick up the tool and use it.

My own fascination with dreams and their meanings came at an early age. The oldest of five children and two working parents, I seldom felt understood or considered for my uniqueness. In my dreams, "I" was the focus. Even in the frightening ones, I got to see how I resolved the conflict. It was a necessary balance to my waking life.

One night, I dreamt the location of something I had misplaced the day before. It amazed me that my subconscious mind had noted the location, even while my attention was focused elsewhere. I wondered what else the subconscious could reveal and read everything I could find on the subject of our dreaming brains.

Many years later, after becoming certified in behavioral therapy, I used dreams to enhance my therapeutic work with clients. Dreams are an incredible shortcut to the psyche. Our dreams are also the art of our soul.

About five years ago, I wrote a letter to Dr. Montague Ullman, clinical professor of psychiatry Emeritus at *Albert Einstein College of Medicine*. He founded the *Dream Laboratory* at the *Maimonides Center* in New York. I discovered his books and couldn't get enough of his writings. To my great delight, he wrote back and suggested a phone call. We exchanged just three letters with each other and two phone calls, but he touched my life profoundly.

He spoke of the value of dream groups, which was a passion for him. I guided dream groups in Los Angeles, New York and Arizona both in University settings and in private homes. I knew the value and benefits—and also the deep and intimate bond that develops among members and the friendships that grew from sharing dreams and helping others to gain perspective on theirs. Monte got a bit emotional when he said that he had never felt more loved than he did in dream group. It was so touching and lovely.

Dr. Ullman passed from this plane on June 7, 2008. He leaves behind a legacy of dream groups around the world. Finland and Sweden were two of his favorites.

My desire is that this volume becomes your daily companion, a place to explore your spirit and know the true nature of your heart. From there you can share your gifts and passions with the world.

May all your cherished dreams come true.

~ Cynthia

Contents

Dedication 5
Acknowledgements 7
Preface 9
Introduction 13

1. UNDERSTANDING THE MEANING OF DREAMS 17

2. THE ANATOMY OF A DREAM 19

3. DREAM LOG 21

4. MY DREAMS 29

5. DREAM SYMBOL GUIDE 229

Suggested Reading 240
Conclusion 241

Introduction

*"Again and again I find that my own inner counselor,
my secret dreaming self, is not only wise
and helpful but usually amusing as well."*
~ SHELDON KOPP,
THE HANGED MAN

Our dreams hold the mystery of our subconscious minds, they bring valuable guidance and inspiration and yet they slip away like the last tinge of color in a summer sunset soon after we wake. The information gleaned in dreams has inspired inventions, medical procedures, music, art, poetry, and all manner of problem solving. It is certainly worth the time to write them down and decipher them.

Journaling has other benefits as well. Very often we repeat themes in our dreams and it is extremely helpful to be able to go back and re-read past dreams of a similar nature. This book is the culmination of over 20 years of dreamwork, listening to dreamers and reading more than 55,000 dreams, thanks mostly to those who sent them to me for the newspaper and magazine columns I've written.

It suggests that you give each dream a title and then enter it in the **"Dream Log"** section (*pg., 21*) with the *date* and *page number*. This allows you to easily keep track and review any dream at any time.

Since we typically dream about what we are involved with in our daily lives, this section has a place for you to write anything that is on your mind, or anything out of the ordinary for that day. This way you don't have to go back and try to remember when something happened. Another area is devoted to your intention or question if you choose to use that feature. You might ask, "What's in my best interest to know about my health at this time?" Or, "What will be the outcome if I take the job offer?" Some nights you may want to ask for guidance, other times you may just want to see what message is delivered without your prompting.

This section also has an area to write the main, strong symbols from your dream. Remember anything can be a symbol, a person, a place, a thing, an action, even feelings, tastes, sounds and smells. There is a place for the date, the title and the dream itself. There's a place to write your interpretation, the insights you gleaned and any action you will take based on the meaning of your dream. Most dreams will fit on the two pages provided, but some may require many pages, so, you can note the page number with the title of each dream on the contents page.

As you use this book, you will be learning more about yourself, your connection to others and to your purpose. Going within is a wonderful journey that will take you to places beyond your imagination.

You may want to collect a few pens in different colors and a flashlight or better yet, light-up pens to make it easy to write your dream down without waking all the way up!

You don't have to write down every dream. As you start paying more attention to them, you'll get a sense for some being more important than others—some are simple, literal reflections of the day. Getting in the habit of writing everyday, however, is a good way to remind your subconscious mind to deliver your dream when you wake.

Anyone who has ever had a meaningful dream knows the tremendous value of our nocturnal dramas. The wisdom of their guidance is not really surprising considering it comes from your own subconscious mind which has recorded every second of your life and from the Creator of life itself. As so eloquently written by Jungian analyst and Episcopal priest, John A. Sanford "Dreams are God's forgotten language."

I've included some common dream symbols and their generally accepted associations (see, *Dream Symbol Guide, pg. 229*). It is best to ask yourself first, what the symbol means to you since each dream has a specific meaning, custom designed for the dreamer. Many people, however, do ascribe the same meanings to many symbols and, when stumped, they can be a good place to begin your detective work.

I've also included a list of some of my favorite dream books (see, *Suggested Reading, pg. 240*). Some are old and still incredibly valid. Thanks to many online sources, used copies can be easy to find.

I'd like to make one last suggestion before you embark on your dream journey of self-discovery. If you have a dream that brings up disturbing memories and you feel the need, please contact a counselor or clergy person for support. Things do bubble up from our past, in my experience nearly always when we are healthy and ready to process and move beyond the effects of trauma. This is another gift our dreams offer, freedom from our past!

So, go forth dreamer and claim your birthright, the beauty and magic of your dreams.

*The future belongs to those who believe in
the beauty of their dreams.*
~ ELEANOR ROOSEVELT,
AMERICAN FIRST LADY

CHAPTER ONE

Understanding the Meaning of Your Dreams

Uncovering the meaning of your dream is different than just interpreting it. Interpreting is like seeing a beautiful scene. You see a tree, gift-wrapped packages, a chubby man in a fur trimmed red suit and you know those items have meaning. The decorated tree is a happy ritual for those who celebrate the holiday. There are gifts in the packages and Santa is a cheerful old elf who brings joy to children young and old. You have interpreted the scene.

Understanding its meaning is like smelling the earthy pine fragrance from the tree, and the cinnamon scented pine cones. It's unwrapping a glitzy box to find the scarf you've been wanting; and it's knowing that Santa is really your Uncle Ralph, dressed up to delight the children. It's like tasting the eggnog and hearing the snaps and pops of the Yule log blazing in the fireplace. It is feeling the joy and love when gathering with family and friends.

Everyone can learn to remember more of their dreams and interpret them. Understanding the meaning takes a bit more effort. It is the art of dreamwork. Anyone can follow a recipe, but some chefs always cook up a more delicious and well-presented meal than others.

To master this art, sit with the dream for a while. Read what you've written about it and bring it vividly to mind. Review the symbols and read your interpretation. Next get inside the symbols, as if you could smell, taste, listen to—whatever senses would be appropriate for each symbol. Put yourself in the scene as if you could participate in it. How do you feel? If this is too frightening because of the nature of the dream, imagine sending in a detective to investigate.

If you have a dream that you are falling, allow yourself to remember the dream and the feeling you had in the dream. It might go like this: *I'm falling. I can't see what is below me. It feels like I am rapidly moving toward a bad landing. At best I'll be badly hurt. I have no control over where I am; I can still move my arms and legs—but they just flail around in mid-air. I feel very anxious and afraid.*

Interpretation: *I am blindly moving downward and I fear a bad ending.*

Meaning: Ask yourself, "Where in my life have I lost control? What is taking me down? In what context can I take back control and release anxiety?" Let's say your answers are, "I've lost control of my time. Between work, the kids, and the house—plus my other obligations and social life; I have no time for me anymore. My over-booked schedule is weighing me down. I could stop some of the club and organization meetings to make more time for my health and well-being. My dream means that I need to be proactive in planning my days and stop putting my needs last."

It is reassuring to know that when you do discern what your dream source wants you to glean, you will get a feeling of "aha!" It feels the same as the certainty you feel when you finally remember a name that had eluded you earlier in the day.

Developing the fine art of understanding dream meanings is worth the effort. It will give you a direct hotline to your source. Just imagine how valuable that is; and to think it is absolutely free and as close as your pillow.

CHAPTER TWO

The Anatomy Of A Dream

M*any things influence our dreams. One remains a much-debated* secret. Consider this and make up your own mind.

Dr. Louis Alfred Maury had a dream; in it he was called before the Tribunal during the French Revolution. He was requested to testify on his own behalf, but the judges were not convinced, and he was sentenced to be executed. Mounting the scaffold, he was blindfolded, tied to a plank and the knife of a guillotine fell—severing his head from his body. Maury woke relieved, and found that the head of his bed board had fallen on his cervical vertebrae; and astonished at how his sleeping mind had incorporated an external stimuli. He began experimenting.

In one test Maury asked his associate to place "eau de cologne" near his nostrils once he was asleep. He dreamt that he was in Cairo in a shop owned by Johann Maria Farina. Fabulous adventures ensued. In another he asked that a drop of water be placed on his forehead. He dreamed he was in Italy perspiring heavily and drinking the white wine of Orvieto to quench his thirst. There were several others each with fascinating results.

Freud was so impressed with Maury's work that he discussed it in his book: *The Interpretation of Dreams*, published in 1900. "Did dreams happen backwards?", he wondered. To explain an external stimulus, did the entire dream happen instantaneously, or did the subconscious mind somehow anticipate the falling of the headboard and, thus, begin the dream story with the headboard falling right on cue?

Many who wake to music playing, report to be dreaming, of dancing or being in a nightclub or concert just prior to waking. I was once asleep in a cabin that had a smoldering fire gaining volume—I was happily asleep dreaming of sitting at a camp fire making s'mores with my Girl Scout troop! Thankfully, someone yelled, "Fire!" and we all piled out into the snow.

So, we know we can weave external stimuli into our dreams, but how do you explain Maury's dream? A friend of mine told me about his dream that his razor was broken and stopped working. A couple of days later it did. He said, "I must have registered a sound from the razor that registered unconsciously."

What do you think?

CHAPTER THREE

Dream Log

How To Title Your Dream For Your "Dream Log"

When choosing the title of your dream, use keywords to describe the main symbols or themes. This will aid you in identifying a similar or related dream in the future that you might want to compare or contrast elements.

If your dream was:

"I dreamt I was in a crowded pool at a very nice hotel. A man with scuba gear bumped into me as he kicked off to swim away. I saw his eyes through his mask, and he seemed to apologize a little. Then a young girl bumped into me as I made my way across the pool. I stopped to be sure she was okay, she was fine and she smiled as she jumped out of my arms to have more fun. I made my way to a stepladder, mounted inside the pool about mid-way across the length. I got out and saw a charming wood-slatted gate that I could go through to get back inside the hotel. There was a shortcut trail two young girls took using stepping-stones through a moss covered landscape. I continued through the gate. I entered the hotel and realized I was on the top floor, the 5th. It was the most opulent area of the hotel. I had to walk through

a guest room to get to the circular stairway to go down to the 4th floor where I was staying. As I walked through the suite, the owner of the resort was on the phone and cleaning the room at the same time. She waved as if to say it was okay for me to walk through. I went down a floor to the 4th and found my room."

Your title could be:

Swimming In Luxury Others Bumped Into Me But I Found My Right Place.

Record the *title* and the *page number* of your dream in the ***Dream Log.***

My Dream Log

Date	Title	Page
Date	Title	Page
Date	Title	Page
Date	Title	Page
Date	Title	Page
Date	Title	Page
Date	Title	Page
Date	Title	Page
Date	Title	Page
Date	Title	Page
Date	Title	Page
Date	Title	Page
Date	Title	Page
Date	Title	Page
Date	Title	Page
Date	Title	Page
Date	Title	Page
Date	Title	Page
Date	Title	Page
Date	Title	Page

Date	Title	Page
Date	Title	Page
Date	Title	Page
Date	Title	Page
Date	Title	Page
Date	Title	Page
Date	Title	Page
Date	Title	Page
Date	Title	Page
Date	Title	Page
Date	Title	Page
Date	Title	Page
Date	Title	Page
Date	Title	Page
Date	Title	Page
Date	Title	Page
Date	Title	Page
Date	Title	Page
Date	Title	Page

Date	Title	Page
Date	Title	Page
Date	Title	Page
Date	Title	Page
Date	Title	Page
Date	Title	Page
Date	Title	Page
Date	Title	Page
Date	Title	Page
Date	Title	Page
Date	Title	Page
Date	Title	Page
Date	Title	Page
Date	Title	Page
Date	Title	Page
Date	Title	Page
Date	Title	Page
Date	Title	Page
Date	Title	Page
Date	Title	Page
Date	Title	Page

Date	Title	Page
Date	Title	Page
Date	Title	Page
Date	Title	Page
Date	Title	Page
Date	Title	Page
Date	Title	Page
Date	Title	Page
Date	Title	Page
Date	Title	Page
Date	Title	Page
Date	Title	Page
Date	Title	Page
Date	Title	Page
Date	Title	Page
Date	Title	Page
Date	Title	Page
Date	Title	Page

Date	Title	Page
Date	Title	Page
Date	Title	Page
Date	Title	Page
Date	Title	Page
Date	Title	Page
Date	Title	Page
Date	Title	Page
Date	Title	Page
Date	Title	Page
Date	Title	Page
Date	Title	Page
Date	Title	Page
Date	Title	Page
Date	Title	Page
Date	Title	Page
Date	Title	Page
Date	Title	Page
Date	Title	Page

CHAPTER FOUR

My Dreams

How To Get The Most Out Of Your Dream Journal Pages

Date: Write the date the night before you go to sleep, as the dream will occur during your sleep. If you feel the dream occurred just before you wake, you may want to add that date, as in: September 14th, morning of 15th.

Anything unusual or outstanding about your day?: Many of our dreams offer observations of and guidance for our daily concerns and activities. Days later, however, you may forget the squabble you had with a co-worker or the praise you received from your child's teacher. To help make the connections, use this section to make note of the things that stand out about your day.

Do you want to set a dream intention? Or ask a question?: Most nights you'll probably want to see what nocturnal dramas come from your dream source. You can, however, also induce a dream with a purpose. An intention could be a desire for a specific type of dream, such as a flying dream, or the invitation to a departed loved-one to visit you in the dream state. A question could be phrased like this: *"What's in my best interest to know about my health at this time?"* Or, *"What direction should I take in guiding my child to take his homework more seriously?"* Writing your intention or question will plant it in your subconscious mind and will help you connect your dreams to your purpose when you interpret your dream.

Write down your dream: *Unlike movies, dreams don't necessarily make logical sense, don't fill in the gaps, just write down what you remember in the order it happened.* In this dream, the girl bumped into the dreamer in the pool and then the girl was jumping out of the dreamer's arms—even though the dreamer didn't see herself pick up the child. Anything is possible in our dream worlds.

Give your dream a title: *Include the main symbols or theme of your dream in the title and write it down.* It will probably be easier to write your dream *first* and then give it a title.

Main symbols and theme of your dream: *Copy the main symbols in your dream here for quick reference.* Ask yourself, "What is the theme of this dream?" and write that here as well. In this dream, the main symbols include: pool, man, girl, gate, shortcut, hotel, stairs, woman, and phone. The theme could be stated as hotel-pool—it's whatever stands out most to the dreamer.

How did the dream make you feel?: *What feeling did you come out of your dream with?* Keep in mind that it may be different than how you feel once you interpret the dream. Often at first glance dreams can be unsettling or frightening. These emotions seem to be a tool used by the subconscious mind to help us remember the dream or pay attention to it. Once you break the dream down and understand its meaning, it becomes appreciated advice, and is usually reassuring.

Your interpretation: *Ask yourself what you associate with each of the main symbols and string together those meanings.* This dreamer told me that she had a vague feeling she had been at the hotel in her dream in a previous dream. That's common and may indicate a continuation of something she is working on in her waking state, either physically, mentally, emotionally or spiritually.

Hotels offer temporary housing—this may be a short-lived issue. Pools and any body of water can relate to emotions. In this dream the dreamer is crowded out by a man dressed in scuba gear and then a young girl. The male was prepared to dive—get deeper into the emotional waters,—which could represent the male aspect of the dreamer.

Traditionally the male aspect of a female, in the language of dreams, has to do with bread-winning, protecting, competition and the like. Here the earning aspect of the dreamer is ready to dive-in and go for it—he has the equipment or tools needed to succeed. Next a young girl bumps into the dreamer. The dreamer is nurturing with the girl and happy that she is unhurt. The girl may represent the child part of the dreamer, the playful, naive, un-jaded aspect.

The dreamer gets herself out of the pool (emotional situation,) and walks through a gate, the intended method of exiting the pool area, and notices two girls who take a shortcut. Next, she is on the top floor (highest position) in a luxurious hotel, and has to walk through a room that is being cleaned to get to the stairway. She passes the owner (authority) who is on the phone (communicating) and gives her permission to pass through. She walks down one flight of stairs to her room. She is just one floor away from the best rooms (situation/conditions) and 4 floors above ground level.

Insights gleaned: *The dreamer has come a long way toward her financial/career goals.* She has not lost her childlike joy in the process. While some "get there" quicker by taking certain shortcuts, she has taken the more traditional path. She is close to the height of luxury or high achievement and comfortable with where she is at the present. The dream is an encouraging one.

Action to be taken: *The dreamer may want to ask a question of her next dream such as, "What is my best next step toward achieving my career and financial goals?"* She may want to observe others who have already accomplished a similar goal to learn from their actions as well.

Date :

Note anything unusual or outstanding about your day.

Do you want to set a dream intention? Or ask a question?

Main symbols and theme of your dream :

How did you feel when you woke from your dream?

Your interpretation :

Insights gleaned :

Action to be taken :

Give Your Dream a Title : _____

> "Judge of your natural
> character by what you do in
> your dreams."
> ~ RALPH WALDO EMERSON,
> AMERICAN WRITER, POET

Date :

Note anything unusual or outstanding about your day.

Do you want to set a dream intention? Or ask a question?

Main symbols and theme of your dream :

How did you feel when you woke from your dream?

Your interpretation :

Insights gleaned :

Action to be taken :

Give Your Dream a Title :

"And He said, 'Hear now my words: If there be a prophet among you, I, the Lord, will make myself known to him in a vision and will speak to him in a dream.'"

~ HOLY BIBLE,
NUMBERS 12:6

Date :

Note anything unusual or outstanding about your day.

Do you want to set a dream intention? Or ask a question?

Main symbols and theme of your dream :

How did you feel when you woke from your dream?

Your interpretation :

Insights gleaned :

Action to be taken :

Give Your Dream a Title :

"Even sleepers are workers and collaborators in what goes on in the Universe."
~HERACLITUS,
GREEK PHILOSOPHER

Date : _____

Note anything unusual or outstanding about your day.

_____
_____
_____

Do you want to set a dream intention? Or ask a question?

_____
_____
_____

Main symbols and theme of your dream :

_____
_____
_____

How did you feel when you woke from your dream?

_____

Your interpretation :

_____
_____
_____

Insights gleaned :

_____
_____
_____

Action to be taken :

_____
_____

Give Your Dream a Title :

"Why does the eye see a thing more clearly in dreams than the imagination when awake."

~ LEONARDO DA VINCI,
ITALIAN ARTIST, SCIENTIST, ARCHITECT.

Date :

Note anything unusual or outstanding about your day.

Do you want to set a dream intention? Or ask a question?

Main symbols and theme of your dream :

How did you feel when you woke from your dream?

Your interpretation :

Insights gleaned :

Action to be taken :

Give Your Dream a Title : _____

> *"What dreaming does is give us the fluidity to enter other worlds by destroying our sense of knowing this world... dreaming is a journey of unthinkable dimensions."*
> ~ CARLOS CASTENADA,
> AMERICAN, ANTHROPOLOGIST, MYSTIC.

Date : _____

Note anything unusual or outstanding about your day.

_____
_____
_____

Do you want to set a dream intention? Or ask a question?

_____
_____
_____

Main symbols and theme of your dream :

_____
_____
_____

How did you feel when you woke from your dream?

_____

Your interpretation :

_____
_____
_____

Insights gleaned :

_____
_____
_____

Action to be taken :

_____
_____

Give Your Dream a Title :

"Dreams are often most profound when they seem the most crazy."
~ SIGMUND FREUD,
THE INTERPRETATION OF DREAMS
1900

Date : _____

Note anything unusual or outstanding about your day.
_____
_____
_____

Do you want to set a dream intention? Or ask a question?
_____
_____
_____

Main symbols and theme of your dream :
_____
_____
_____

How did you feel when you woke from your dream?
_____

Your interpretation :
_____
_____
_____

Insights gleaned :
_____
_____
_____

Action to be taken :
_____
_____

Give Your Dream a Title : ....

"Existence would be intolerable if we were never to dream."
~ ANATOLÉ FRANCE,
FRENCH NOVELIST

Date :

Note anything unusual or outstanding about your day.

Do you want to set a dream intention? Or ask a question?

Main symbols and theme of your dream :

How did you feel when you woke from your dream?

Your interpretation :

Insights gleaned :

Action to be taken :

Give Your Dream a Title :

"The soul in sleep gives proof
of its divine nature."
~ CICERO,
ROMAN PHILOSOPHER

Date :

Note anything unusual or outstanding about your day.

Do you want to set a dream intention? Or ask a question?

Main symbols and theme of your dream :

How did you feel when you woke from your dream?

Your interpretation :

Insights gleaned :

Action to be taken :

Give Your Dream a Title :

> "I am against nature. I don't dig nature at all. I think nature is very unnatural. I think the truly natural things are dreams, which nature can't touch with decay."
> ~ BOB DYLAN,
> AMERICAN SINGER/SONGWRITER.

Date :

Note anything unusual or outstanding about your day.

Do you want to set a dream intention? Or ask a question?

Main symbols and theme of your dream :

How did you feel when you woke from your dream?

Your interpretation :

Insights gleaned :

Action to be taken :

Give Your Dream a Title :

> "There couldn't be a society
> of people who didn't dream.
> They'd be dead in two weeks."
> ~ WILLIAM BURROUGHS,
> AMERICAN AUTHOR

Date :

Note anything unusual or outstanding about your day.

Do you want to set a dream intention? Or ask a question?

Main symbols and theme of your dream :

How did you feel when you woke from your dream?

Your interpretation :

Insights gleaned :

Action to be taken :

Give Your Dream a Title :

> *"If someone were to tell me I had twenty years left, and ask me how I'd like to spend them, I'd reply 'Give me two hours of activity and I'll take the other twenty-two in dreams.'"*
>
> ~ LUIS BUNUEL,
> SPANISH FILM-MAKER, SURREALIST

Date : _____

Note anything unusual or outstanding about your day.

_____
_____
_____

Do you want to set a dream intention? Or ask a question?

_____
_____
_____

Main symbols and theme of your dream :

_____
_____
_____

How did you feel when you woke from your dream?

_____

Your interpretation :

_____
_____
_____

Insights gleaned :

_____
_____
_____

Action to be taken :

_____
_____

Give Your Dream a Title : _____

> "Sleep hath it's own world,
> And a wide realm of wild
> reality, And dreams in their
> development have breath,
> And tears and tortures, and
> the touch of joy"
> ~ LORD BYRON,
> THE DREAM, ENGLISH POET

Date :

Note anything unusual or outstanding about your day.

Do you want to set a dream intention? Or ask a question?

Main symbols and theme of your dream :

How did you feel when you woke from your dream?

Your interpretation :

Insights gleaned :

Action to be taken :

Give Your Dream a Title :

"If a little dreaming is
dangerous, the cure for
it is not to dream less,
but to dream more,
to dream all the time."
~ MARCEL PROUST,
REMEMBRANCE OF THINGS PAST,
FRENCH NOVELIST

Date :

Note anything unusual or outstanding about your day.

Do you want to set a dream intention? Or ask a question?

Main symbols and theme of your dream :

How did you feel when you woke from your dream?

Your interpretation :

Insights gleaned :

Action to be taken :

Give Your Dream a Title : ....

> "I never can decide whether
> my dreams are the result of
> my thoughts, or my thoughts
> are the result of my dreams."
> ~ D.H. LAWRENCE,
> ENGLISH NOVELIST

Date : _____

Note anything unusual or outstanding about your day.

_____
_____
_____

Do you want to set a dream intention? Or ask a question?

_____
_____
_____

Main symbols and theme of your dream :

_____
_____
_____

How did you feel when you woke from your dream?

Your interpretation :

_____
_____
_____

Insights gleaned :

_____
_____
_____

Action to be taken :

_____
_____

Give Your Dream a Title :

> "As I live and am a man, this is an unexaggerated tale — my dreams become the substance of my life."
> ~Samuel T. Coleridge,
> English Poet, Philosopher

Date :

Note anything unusual or outstanding about your day.

Do you want to set a dream intention? Or ask a question?

Main symbols and theme of your dream :

How did you feel when you woke from your dream?

Your interpretation :

Insights gleaned :

Action to be taken :

Give Your Dream a Title :

> "Maybe the wildest dreams are but the needful preludes of the truth."
> ~ ALFRED LORD TENNYSON,
> ENGLISH POET

Date :

Note anything unusual or outstanding about your day.

Do you want to set a dream intention? Or ask a question?

Main symbols and theme of your dream :

How did you feel when you woke from your dream?

Your interpretation :

Insights gleaned :

Action to be taken :

Give Your Dream a Title : _____

"*Let us learn to dream,
gentlemen, and then we may
perhaps find the truth.*"
~ F.A. KEULE,
GERMAN CHEMIST, DISCOVERER OF
THE STRUCTURE OF BENZENE IN A
DREAM

Date : _____

Note anything unusual or outstanding about your day.

Do you want to set a dream intention? Or ask a question?

Main symbols and theme of your dream :

How did you feel when you woke from your dream?

Your interpretation :

Insights gleaned :

Action to be taken :

Give Your Dream a Title : _____

"We are such stuff as dreams are made on,"
~ WILLIAM SHAKESPEARE,
16TH CENTURY POET/PLAYWRIGHT

Date :

Note anything unusual or outstanding about your day.

Do you want to set a dream intention? Or ask a question?

Main symbols and theme of your dream :

How did you feel when you woke from your dream?

Your interpretation :

Insights gleaned :

Action to be taken :

Give Your Dream a Title : _____

"A dream is a little hidden door in the innermost and most secret recesses of the soul, opening into that cosmic night which was psyche long before there was any ego-consciousness."

~ CARL JUNG,
PSYCHIATRIST & PSYCHOLOGIST

Date : _____

Note anything unusual or outstanding about your day.

_____
_____
_____
_____

Do you want to set a dream intention? Or ask a question?

_____
_____
_____
_____

Main symbols and theme of your dream :

_____
_____
_____
_____

How did you feel when you woke from your dream?

_____

Your interpretation :

_____
_____
_____
_____

Insights gleaned :

_____
_____
_____
_____

Action to be taken :

_____
_____
_____

Give Your Dream a Title : ....

> "In dreams we catch glimpses
> of a life larger than our
> own... For one fleeting night
> a princelier nature captures
> us and we become as great as
> our aspirations."
> ~ HELEN KELLER,
> AMERICAN WRITER

Date : _____

Note anything unusual or outstanding about your day.

_____
_____
_____

Do you want to set a dream intention? Or ask a question?

_____
_____
_____

Main symbols and theme of your dream :

_____
_____
_____

How did you feel when you woke from your dream?

_____

Your interpretation :

_____
_____
_____

Insights gleaned :

_____
_____
_____

Action to be taken :

_____
_____

Give Your Dream a Title :

> "It is very queer. But my dreams make conclusions for me. They decide things finally. I dream a decision."
> ~D.H. Lawrence,
> English Novelist

Date :

Note anything unusual or outstanding about your day.

Do you want to set a dream intention? Or ask a question?

Main symbols and theme of your dream :

How did you feel when you woke from your dream?

Your interpretation :

Insights gleaned :

Action to be taken :

Give Your Dream a Title :

"All our dreams can come true, if we have the courage to pursue them."
~ WALT DISNEY,
AMERICAN CARTOONIST,
PRODUCER, THEME PARK DESIGNER

Date :

Note anything unusual or outstanding about your day.

Do you want to set a dream intention? Or ask a question?

Main symbols and theme of your dream :

How did you feel when you woke from your dream?

Your interpretation :

Insights gleaned :

Action to be taken :

Give Your Dream a Title :

*"Dreams are
necessary to life."*
~ Anais Nin,
French Author

Date :

Note anything unusual or outstanding about your day.

Do you want to set a dream intention? Or ask a question?

Main symbols and theme of your dream :

How did you feel when you woke from your dream?

Your interpretation :

Insights gleaned :

Action to be taken :

Give Your Dream a Title :

> "Dreams are the touchstones of our character."
> ~ HENRY DAVID THOREAU,
> AMERICAN AUTHOR, POET

Date : _____

Note anything unusual or outstanding about your day.

_____
_____
_____

Do you want to set a dream intention? Or ask a question?

_____
_____
_____

Main symbols and theme of your dream :

_____
_____
_____

How did you feel when you woke from your dream?

Your interpretation :

_____
_____
_____
_____

Insights gleaned :

_____
_____
_____

Action to be taken :

_____
_____

Give Your Dream a Title :

> "Dreams are today's answers
> to tomorrow's questions."
> ~ EDGAR CAYCE,
> AMERICAN MYSTIC, PSYCHIC

Date :

Note anything unusual or outstanding about your day.

Do you want to set a dream intention? Or ask a question?

Main symbols and theme of your dream :

How did you feel when you woke from your dream?

Your interpretation :

Insights gleaned :

Action to be taken :

Give Your Dream a Title : _____

"All the things one has forgotten scream for help in dreams."
~ ELIAS CANETTI,
BULGARIAN NOVELIST

Date : _____

Note anything unusual or outstanding about your day.

Do you want to set a dream intention? Or ask a question?

Main symbols and theme of your dream :

How did you feel when you woke from your dream?

Your interpretation :

Insights gleaned :

Action to be taken :

Give Your Dream a Title :

> "If you take responsibility for yourself you will develop a hunger to accomplish your dreams."
> ~ LES BROWN,
> AMERICAN AUTHOR

Date :

Note anything unusual or outstanding about your day.

Do you want to set a dream intention? Or ask a question?

Main symbols and theme of your dream :

How did you feel when you woke from your dream?

Your interpretation :

Insights gleaned :

Action to be taken :

Give Your Dream a Title :

"The sun god Ra appeared in a dream to a young Egyptian prince and told him he would one day rule Egypt… The prince went on to become Pharaoh Thotmes IV…"
~ Brian Innes,
The Book of Dreams

Date :

Note anything unusual or outstanding about your day.

Do you want to set a dream intention? Or ask a question?

Main symbols and theme of your dream :

How did you feel when you woke from your dream?

Your interpretation :

Insights gleaned :

Action to be taken :

Give Your Dream a Title :

"Living in dreams of yesterday, we find ourselves still dreaming of impossible future conquests."
~ CHARLES LINDBERGH, AMERICAN AVIATOR

Date :

Note anything unusual or outstanding about your day.

Do you want to set a dream intention? Or ask a question?

Main symbols and theme of your dream :

How did you feel when you woke from your dream?

Your interpretation :

Insights gleaned :

Action to be taken :

Give Your Dream a Title :

*"Myths are public dreams,
dreams are private myths."*
~ JOSEPH CAMPBELL,
AMERICAN PHILOSOPHER

Date :

Note anything unusual or outstanding about your day.

Do you want to set a dream intention? Or ask a question?

Main symbols and theme of your dream :

How did you feel when you woke from your dream?

Your interpretation :

Insights gleaned :

Action to be taken :

Give Your Dream a Title : _____

*"One of the most adventurous
things left us is to go to bed.
For no one can lay a hand on
our dreams."*

~ E. V. LUCAS,
ENGLISH WRITER

Date : _____

Note anything unusual or outstanding about your day.

_____
_____
_____

Do you want to set a dream intention? Or ask a question?

_____
_____
_____

Main symbols and theme of your dream :

_____
_____
_____

How did you feel when you woke from your dream?

_____

Your interpretation :

_____
_____
_____

Insights gleaned :

_____
_____
_____

Action to be taken :

_____
_____

Give Your Dream a Title : _____

"Our truest life is when we are in dreams awake."
~ Henry David Thoreau,
American Author, Poet

Date :

Note anything unusual or outstanding about your day.

Do you want to set a dream intention? Or ask a question?

Main symbols and theme of your dream :

How did you feel when you woke from your dream?

Your interpretation :

Insights gleaned :

Action to be taken :

Give Your Dream a Title :

*"Reality is wrong.
Dreams are for real."*
~ TUPAC SHAKUR,
AMERICAN RAPPER

Date : _____

Note anything unusual or outstanding about your day.

_____
_____
_____

Do you want to set a dream intention? Or ask a question?

_____
_____
_____

Main symbols and theme of your dream :

_____
_____
_____

How did you feel when you woke from your dream?

Your interpretation :

_____
_____
_____

Insights gleaned :

_____
_____
_____

Action to be taken :

_____
_____

Give Your Dream a Title :

> "So many of our dreams at first seem impossible, then they seem improbable, and then, when we summon the will, they soon become inevitable."
>
> ~ CHRISTOPHER REEVE,
> AMERICAN ACTOR

Date :

Note anything unusual or outstanding about your day.

Do you want to set a dream intention? Or ask a question?

Main symbols and theme of your dream :

How did you feel when you woke from your dream?

Your interpretation :

Insights gleaned :

Action to be taken :

Give Your Dream a Title : _____

> "Some men see things as they are and say, 'why?' I dream things that never were and say why not."
> ~ ROBERT KENNEDY,
> U.S. ATTORNEY GENERAL

Date :

Note anything unusual or outstanding about your day.

Do you want to set a dream intention? Or ask a question?

Main symbols and theme of your dream :

How did you feel when you woke from your dream?

Your interpretation :

Insights gleaned :

Action to be taken :

Give Your Dream a Title :

> "Man, alone, has the power to transform his thoughts into physical reality; man, alone, can dream and make his dreams come true."
> ~ NAPOLEON HILL,
> AMERICAN AUTHOR

Date : _____

Note anything unusual or outstanding about your day.

_____
_____
_____

Do you want to set a dream intention? Or ask a question?

_____
_____
_____

Main symbols and theme of your dream :

_____
_____
_____

How did you feel when you woke from your dream?

_____

Your interpretation :

_____
_____
_____

Insights gleaned :

_____
_____
_____

Action to be taken :

_____
_____

Give Your Dream a Title :

> "The best book on dreams you will ever read is the one you write yourself."
> ~ Hugh Lynn Cayce,
> President of the A.R.E.

Date : _____

Note anything unusual or outstanding about your day.

Do you want to set a dream intention? Or ask a question?

Main symbols and theme of your dream :

How did you feel when you woke from your dream?

Your interpretation :

Insights gleaned :

Action to be taken :

Give Your Dream a Title :

> "Dreams are to our waking experiences as the moon is to the sun, providing a special intensifying nocturnal light."
> ~ SHELDON KOPP,
> AMERICAN PSYCHOTHERAPIST, AUTHOR

Date : _____

Note anything unusual or outstanding about your day.

_____
_____
_____

Do you want to set a dream intention? Or ask a question?

_____
_____
_____

Main symbols and theme of your dream :

_____
_____
_____

How did you feel when you woke from your dream?

Your interpretation :

_____
_____
_____

Insights gleaned :

_____
_____
_____

Action to be taken :

_____
_____

Give Your Dream a Title : _____

> "They tease me now, telling me it was only a dream. But does it matter whether it was a dream or reality, if the dream made known to me the truth."
>
> ~ FEODOR DOSTOYEVSKY,
> RUSSIAN AUTHOR

Date :

Note anything unusual or outstanding about your day.

Do you want to set a dream intention? Or ask a question?

Main symbols and theme of your dream :

How did you feel when you woke from your dream?

Your interpretation :

Insights gleaned :

Action to be taken :

Give Your Dream a Title :

> "The whole dreamwork is essentially subjective, and a dream is a theater in which the dreamer is himself the scene, the player the prompter, the producer, the author, the public and the critic."
> ~ CARL JUNG,
> PSYCHIATRIST & PSYCHOLOGIST

Date :

Note anything unusual or outstanding about your day.

Do you want to set a dream intention? Or ask a question?

Main symbols and theme of your dream :

How did you feel when you woke from your dream?

Your interpretation :

Insights gleaned :

Action to be taken :

Give Your Dream a Title : _____

"In dreams we see ourselves naked and acting out our real characters, even more clearly than we see others awake.

~ HENRY DAVID THOREAU,
AMERICAN AUTHOR, POET

Date :

Note anything unusual or outstanding about your day.

Do you want to set a dream intention? Or ask a question?

Main symbols and theme of your dream :

How did you feel when you woke from your dream?

Your interpretation :

Insights gleaned :

Action to be taken :

Give Your Dream a Title : _____

"Sharing our dreams with
others is sharing ourselves
and enables us to know each
other deeply."
~Dick McLeester,
Author,
Welcome to the Magic Theater

Date :

Note anything unusual or outstanding about your day.

Do you want to set a dream intention? Or ask a question?

Main symbols and theme of your dream :

How did you feel when you woke from your dream?

Your interpretation :

Insights gleaned :

Action to be taken :

Give Your Dream a Title :

"What is now proved was
once only imagin'd."
~ WILLIAM BLAKE,
ENGLISH ARTIST AND POET

Date :

Note anything unusual or outstanding about your day.

Do you want to set a dream intention? Or ask a question?

Main symbols and theme of your dream :

How did you feel when you woke from your dream?

Your interpretation :

Insights gleaned :

Action to be taken :

Give Your Dream a Title :

"Take, if you must this little bag of dreams, unloose the cord, and they will wrap you round."
~ WILLIAM BUTLER YEATS,
IRISH POET

Date : _____

Note anything unusual or outstanding about your day.

Do you want to set a dream intention? Or ask a question?

Main symbols and theme of your dream :

How did you feel when you woke from your dream?

Your interpretation :

Insights gleaned :

Action to be taken :

Give Your Dream a Title : _____

"In all of us, even in good men there is a lawless, wild beast nature, which peers out in sleep."
~SOCRATES,
GREEK PHILOSOPHER

Date :

Note anything unusual or outstanding about your day.

Do you want to set a dream intention? Or ask a question?

Main symbols and theme of your dream :

How did you feel when you woke from your dream?

Your interpretation :

Insights gleaned :

Action to be taken :

Give Your Dream a Title :

> "I arise from dreams of thee in
> the first sweet sleep of night."
> ~ PERCY BYSSHE SHELLEY,
> ENGLISH POET

Date :

Note anything unusual or outstanding about your day.

Do you want to set a dream intention? Or ask a question?

Main symbols and theme of your dream :

How did you feel when you woke from your dream?

Your interpretation :

Insights gleaned :

Action to be taken :

Give Your Dream a Title :

> "I was not looking for my dreams to interpret my life, but rather for my life to interpret my dreams."
> ~ SUSAN SONTAG,
> AMERICAN WRITER

Date : _____

Note anything unusual or outstanding about your day.

Do you want to set a dream intention? Or ask a question?

Main symbols and theme of your dream :

How did you feel when you woke from your dream?

Your interpretation :

Insights gleaned :

Action to be taken :

Give Your Dream a Title :

> "He whose talk is of oxen will
> probably dream of oxen."
> ~ Thomas de Quincey,
> English writer

Date :

Note anything unusual or outstanding about your day.

Do you want to set a dream intention? Or ask a question?

Main symbols and theme of your dream :

How did you feel when you woke from your dream?

Your interpretation :

Insights gleaned :

Action to be taken :

Give Your Dream a Title :

> "There have been times in my life when I have fallen asleep in tears; but in my dreams the most charming forms have come to console and cheer me, and I have risen the next morning fresh and joyful."
> ~ JOHANN WOLFGANG VON GOETHE, GERMAN POET

Date :

Note anything unusual or outstanding about your day.

Do you want to set a dream intention? Or ask a question?

Main symbols and theme of your dream :

How did you feel when you woke from your dream?

Your interpretation :

Insights gleaned :

Action to be taken :

Give Your Dream a Title :

"Each dream is unique, like each sunrise, with different feelings, textures and colors."

~ FARIBA BOGZARAN,
VISIONARY, PROFESSOR, ARTIST,
PIONEER IN DREAM STUDIES,
PAINTING DREAM IMAGES

Date : ....

Note anything unusual or outstanding about your day.

_____
_____
_____

Do you want to set a dream intention? Or ask a question?

_____
_____
_____

Main symbols and theme of your dream :

_____
_____
_____

How did you feel when you woke from your dream?

_____

Your interpretation :

_____
_____
_____

Insights gleaned :

_____
_____
_____

Action to be taken :

_____
_____
_____

Give Your Dream a Title :

"That we come to this earth to
live is untrue; We come but to
sleep, to dream."
~ Aztec Poem

Date : _____

Note anything unusual or outstanding about your day.

Do you want to set a dream intention? Or ask a question?

Main symbols and theme of your dream :

How did you feel when you woke from your dream?

Your interpretation :

Insights gleaned :

Action to be taken :

Give Your Dream a Title : _____

"Sleep offers itself to all: it is an oracle always ready to be our infallible and silent counselor."
~ SYNESIUS OF CYRENE

Date :

Note anything unusual or outstanding about your day.

Do you want to set a dream intention? Or ask a question?

Main symbols and theme of your dream :

How did you feel when you woke from your dream?

Your interpretation :

Insights gleaned :

Action to be taken :

Give Your Dream a Title :

> "Dreams of one's own death almost always reflect the fact that we have reached the point of being willing to relinquish our old roles and self-images, and for this reason these are often the most important dreams of all."
> ~ ANN FARADAY,
> THE DREAM GAME

Date :

Note anything unusual or outstanding about your day.

Do you want to set a dream intention? Or ask a question?

Main symbols and theme of your dream :

How did you feel when you woke from your dream?

Your interpretation :

Insights gleaned :

Action to be taken :

Give Your Dream a Title :

> "Not only is our power of imagination greater in our sleep than in our waking life, but the innate striving for health and happiness often assert themselves in our sleep more forcefully than when we are awake."
>
> ~ ERIC FROMM,
> AMERICAN PSYCHOANALYST

Date :

Note anything unusual or outstanding about your day.

Do you want to set a dream intention? Or ask a question?

Main symbols and theme of your dream :

How did you feel when you woke from your dream?

Your interpretation :

Insights gleaned :

Action to be taken :

Give Your Dream a Title :

> "A person who dreams lives long."
> ~ FLORINDA DONNER,
> AMERICAN AUTHOR,
> ANTHROPOLOGIST

Date :

Note anything unusual or outstanding about your day.

Do you want to set a dream intention? Or ask a question?

Main symbols and theme of your dream :

How did you feel when you woke from your dream?

Your interpretation :

Insights gleaned :

Action to be taken :

Give Your Dream a Title :

> "Dreams may seem as fragile
> and floating as silk chiffon,
> but they are never-the-less
> sturdy props for easing
> our way."
> ~ Patricia Garfield,
> American Psychologist

Date : _____

Note anything unusual or outstanding about your day.
_____
_____
_____

Do you want to set a dream intention? Or ask a question?
_____
_____
_____

Main symbols and theme of your dream :
_____
_____
_____

How did you feel when you woke from your dream?
_____

Your interpretation :
_____
_____
_____

Insights gleaned :
_____
_____
_____

Action to be taken :
_____
_____

Give Your Dream a Title :

"We are asleep with compasses
in our hands."
~ W. S. Merwin,
American poet

Date : _____

Note anything unusual or outstanding about your day.

_____
_____
_____

Do you want to set a dream intention? Or ask a question?

_____
_____
_____

Main symbols and theme of your dream :

_____
_____

How did you feel when you woke from your dream?

_____

Your interpretation :

_____
_____
_____

Insights gleaned :

_____
_____
_____

Action to be taken :

_____
_____

Give Your Dream a Title : _____

"All that we see or seem, is but a dream within a dream."
~ EDGAR ALLAN POE,
AMERICAN WRITER

Date :

Note anything unusual or outstanding about your day.

Do you want to set a dream intention? Or ask a question?

Main symbols and theme of your dream :

How did you feel when you woke from your dream?

Your interpretation :

Insights gleaned :

Action to be taken :

Give Your Dream a Title :

> "The symbol in the dream has more the value of a parable: it does not conceal it teachers."
> ~ CARL JUNG,
> PSYCHOLOGICAL REFLECTIONS

Date :

Note anything unusual or outstanding about your day.

Do you want to set a dream intention? Or ask a question?

Main symbols and theme of your dream :

How did you feel when you woke from your dream?

Your interpretation :

Insights gleaned :

Action to be taken :

Give Your Dream a Title : _____

> *"If there is something hauntingly beautiful or impressive in your dream, just honor it, respect it, recall it, sense it with your body. More will come."*
> ~ EUGENE GENDLIN,
> LET YOUR BODY INTERPRET YOUR DREAMS

Date : _____

Note anything unusual or outstanding about your day.

Do you want to set a dream intention? Or ask a question?

Main symbols and theme of your dream :

How did you feel when you woke from your dream?

Your interpretation :

Insights gleaned :

Action to be taken :

Give Your Dream a Title :

"It is in our idleness, in our dreams, that the submerged truth sometimes comes to the top."
~ Virginia Woolf,
English Author

Date : _____

Note anything unusual or outstanding about your day.

Do you want to set a dream intention? Or ask a question?

Main symbols and theme of your dream :

How did you feel when you woke from your dream?

Your interpretation :

Insights gleaned :

Action to be taken :

Give Your Dream a Title :

> *"In some ways, your dreams may speak a universal language, and therefore they belong not only to you but to a larger community. Others may find wisdom for themselves in your dream."*
> ~LOUIS M. SAVARY,
> AMERICAN WRITER & SCHOLAR

Date : _____

Note anything unusual or outstanding about your day.

Do you want to set a dream intention? Or ask a question?

Main symbols and theme of your dream :

How did you feel when you woke from your dream?

Your interpretation :

Insights gleaned :

Action to be taken :

Give Your Dream a Title : _____

"All human beings are also dream beings. Dreaming ties all mankind together."
~Jack Kerouac,
Canadian born, American writer

Date :

Note anything unusual or outstanding about your day.

Do you want to set a dream intention? Or ask a question?

Main symbols and theme of your dream :

How did you feel when you woke from your dream?

Your interpretation :

Insights gleaned :

Action to be taken :

Give Your Dream a Title : _____

> "Because dreams come from the unconscious, they share the same language of symbolism as art, myths, folklore, and religious ritual, which all spring from the imagination."
> ~ KAREN A. SIGNELL,
> AMERICAN PSYCHOLOGIST AND WRITER

Date : _____

Note anything unusual or outstanding about your day.

_____
_____
_____

Do you want to set a dream intention? Or ask a question?

_____
_____
_____

Main symbols and theme of your dream :

_____
_____
_____

How did you feel when you woke from your dream?

_____

Your interpretation :

_____
_____
_____

Insights gleaned :

_____
_____
_____

Action to be taken :

_____
_____

Give Your Dream a Title :

> "One of the characteristics
> of the dream is that nothing
> surprises us in it."
> ~ JEAN COCTEAU,
> FRENCH WRITER & FILMMAKER

Date : _____

Note anything unusual or outstanding about your day.

Do you want to set a dream intention? Or ask a question?

Main symbols and theme of your dream :

How did you feel when you woke from your dream?

Your interpretation :

Insights gleaned :

Action to be taken :

Give Your Dream a Title :

> "Our dreams are firsthand creations, rather than residues of waking life. We have the capacity for infinite creativity; at least while dreaming, we partake of the power of the immanent Spirit, the infinite Godhead that creates the cosmos."
>
> ~ GORDON GLOBUS,
> AMERICAN PSYCHIATRIST & WRITER

Date : _____

Note anything unusual or outstanding about your day.

Do you want to set a dream intention? Or ask a question?

Main symbols and theme of your dream :

How did you feel when you woke from your dream?

Your interpretation :

Insights gleaned :

Action to be taken :

Give Your Dream a Title : _____

"Imagination is more
important than knowledge."
~ ALBERT EINSTEIN,
GERMAN BORN, AMERICAN
PHYSICIST

Date : _____

Note anything unusual or outstanding about your day.

_____
_____
_____

Do you want to set a dream intention? Or ask a question?

_____
_____

Main symbols and theme of your dream :

_____
_____

How did you feel when you woke from your dream?

Your interpretation :

_____
_____
_____

Insights gleaned :

_____
_____

Action to be taken :

_____
_____

Give Your Dream a Title :

> "We do not feel as if we were producing the dreams, it is rather as if the dreams come to us. They are not subject to our control but obey their own laws."
> ~ CARL JUNG,
> PSYCHOLOGICAL REFLECTIONS

Date : _____

Note anything unusual or outstanding about your day.

_____
_____
_____

Do you want to set a dream intention? Or ask a question?

_____
_____
_____

Main symbols and theme of your dream :

_____
_____
_____

How did you feel when you woke from your dream?

_____

Your interpretation :

_____
_____
_____

Insights gleaned :

_____
_____
_____

Action to be taken :

_____
_____

Give Your Dream a Title : _____

> "It is important that we learn to feel comfortable leaving some dreams a mystery. There will be other dreams and there will always be some mystery remaining."
> ~Dick Leester,
> Welcome to the Magic Theater

Date : _____

Note anything unusual or outstanding about your day.

Do you want to set a dream intention? Or ask a question?

Main symbols and theme of your dream :

How did you feel when you woke from your dream?

Your interpretation :

Insights gleaned :

Action to be taken :

Give Your Dream a Title :

> "Dreaming is the opportunity to hold a citizenship in two worlds, equally real but with different logic and limitations."
> ~ WILLIAM DEMENT,
> THE SLEEP WALKERS

Date :

Note anything unusual or outstanding about your day.

Do you want to set a dream intention? Or ask a question?

Main symbols and theme of your dream :

How did you feel when you woke from your dream?

Your interpretation :

Insights gleaned :

Action to be taken :

Give Your Dream a Title : _____

> *"If we believe in the Bible, we must accept the fact, that, in the old days, God and his angels came to humans in their sleep and made themselves known in their dreams."*
>
> ~ABRAHAM LINCOLN,
> AMERICAN PRESIDENT

Date :

Note anything unusual or outstanding about your day.

Do you want to set a dream intention? Or ask a question?

Main symbols and theme of your dream :

How did you feel when you woke from your dream?

Your interpretation :

Insights gleaned :

Action to be taken :

Give Your Dream a Title :

> *"A dream is a personal document, a letter to oneself."*
> ~Calvin Hall,
> The Meaning of Dreams

Date : _____

Note anything unusual or outstanding about your day.

_____
_____
_____

Do you want to set a dream intention? Or ask a question?

_____
_____
_____

Main symbols and theme of your dream :

_____
_____
_____

How did you feel when you woke from your dream?

_____

Your interpretation :

_____
_____
_____

Insights gleaned :

_____
_____
_____

Action to be taken :

_____
_____

Give Your Dream a Title :

> "There is a dream dreaming us."
> ~ A Kalahari San Person,
> quoted by Joseph Campbell

Date : _____

Note anything unusual or outstanding about your day.

Do you want to set a dream intention? Or ask a question?

Main symbols and theme of your dream :

How did you feel when you woke from your dream?

Your interpretation :

Insights gleaned :

Action to be taken :

Give Your Dream a Title :

"Just as the waters of earth swell and recede, so our dreams change over time."
~Patricia Garfield,
American Author

Date : ....

Note anything unusual or outstanding about your day.

Do you want to set a dream intention? Or ask a question?

Main symbols and theme of your dream :

How did you feel when you woke from your dream?

Your interpretation :

Insights gleaned :

Action to be taken :

Give Your Dream a Title :

"We do not sleep merely to
live, but to learn to live well."
~Synesius of Cyrene

Date :

Note anything unusual or outstanding about your day.

Do you want to set a dream intention? Or ask a question?

Main symbols and theme of your dream :

How did you feel when you woke from your dream?

Your interpretation :

Insights gleaned :

Action to be taken :

Give Your Dream a Title :

> "...dreams should rightly be regarded as God's forgotten language, or the voice of God."
> ~John A. Sanford,
> Episcopal priest, Author

Date :

Note anything unusual or outstanding about your day.

Do you want to set a dream intention? Or ask a question?

Main symbols and theme of your dream :

How did you feel when you woke from your dream?

Your interpretation :

Insights gleaned :

Action to be taken :

Give Your Dream a Title :

> "[A dream] contains, ... the most valuable of all the discoveries it has been my good fortune to make. Insight such as this falls to one's lot but once in a lifetime."
> ~ SIGMUND FREUD,
> AUSTRIAN PSYCHIATRIST

Date : _____

Note anything unusual or outstanding about your day.

Do you want to set a dream intention? Or ask a question?

Main symbols and theme of your dream :

How did you feel when you woke from your dream?

Your interpretation :

Insights gleaned :

Action to be taken :

Give Your Dream a Title :

"The size of things in dreams will often be determined by factors such as their importance in our lives."
~ Prospero's Library, ©1994 Duncan Baird

Date : ....

Note anything unusual or outstanding about your day.

Do you want to set a dream intention? Or ask a question?

Main symbols and theme of your dream :

How did you feel when you woke from your dream?

Your interpretation :

Insights gleaned :

Action to be taken :

Give Your Dream a Title : _____

"Of scenes of Nature, fields and mountains, Of skies so beauteous after a storm and at night the moon to unearthly bright, …I dream, I dream, I dream."

~ WALT WHITMAN,
AMERICAN POET, JOURNALIST

Date :

Note anything unusual or outstanding about your day.

Do you want to set a dream intention? Or ask a question?

Main symbols and theme of your dream :

How did you feel when you woke from your dream?

Your interpretation :

Insights gleaned :

Action to be taken :

Give Your Dream a Title :

"Dreams are a conversation between the unconscious and the conscious levels of the mind—levels that speak subtly different languages."
~ DAVID FONTANA, PHD,
AMERICAN AUTHOR

Date : _____

Note anything unusual or outstanding about your day.

_____
_____
_____

Do you want to set a dream intention? Or ask a question?

_____
_____
_____

Main symbols and theme of your dream :

_____
_____
_____

How did you feel when you woke from your dream?

Your interpretation :

_____
_____
_____
_____

Insights gleaned :

_____
_____
_____

Action to be taken :

_____
_____

Give Your Dream a Title : ....

> "The experience of dreaming...affords a growth enhancing encounter with other aspects of ourselves."
> ~ MONTAGUE ULLMAN & NAN ZIMMERMAN, CO-AUTHORS: WORKING WITH DREAMS

Date :

Note anything unusual or outstanding about your day.

Do you want to set a dream intention? Or ask a question?

Main symbols and theme of your dream :

How did you feel when you woke from your dream?

Your interpretation :

Insights gleaned :

Action to be taken :

Give Your Dream a Title :

> *"Our dreams are most peculiarly independent of our consciousness and exceedingly valuable because they cannot cheat."*
> ~ CARL JUNG,
> PSYCHIATRIST & PSYCHOLOGIST

Date : _____

Note anything unusual or outstanding about your day.

_____
_____
_____

Do you want to set a dream intention? Or ask a question?

_____
_____
_____

Main symbols and theme of your dream :

_____
_____
_____

How did you feel when you woke from your dream?

_____

Your interpretation :

_____
_____
_____

Insights gleaned :

_____
_____
_____

Action to be taken :

_____
_____
_____

Give Your Dream a Title : _____

"My wish for you is that your night vision will improve to 20/20 for all of the exciting night's that lie ahead for you."

~Robert L. Van de Castle, PhD, Former Director Of The Sleep And Dream Laboratory At The University Of Virginia Medical School

Date : _____

Note anything unusual or outstanding about your day.

Do you want to set a dream intention? Or ask a question?

Main symbols and theme of your dream :

How did you feel when you woke from your dream?

Your interpretation :

Insights gleaned :

Action to be taken :

Give Your Dream a Title :

> *"All of us dream whether we remember dreaming or not. We dream as infants and continue dreaming until we die. Every night we enter an unknown world."*
>
> ~ Tenzin Wangyal Rinpoche,
> The Tibetan Yogas of Dream and Sleep

Date : _____

Note anything unusual or outstanding about your day.

Do you want to set a dream intention? Or ask a question?

Main symbols and theme of your dream :

How did you feel when you woke from your dream?

Your interpretation :

Insights gleaned :

Action to be taken :

Give Your Dream a Title :

> "When and if we are able to understand things from a dog's point of view, we may discover that dogs have a dream life every bit as significant as our own and one that serves some very useful purpose to the dog's life"
>
> ~ Dr. Alan Beck,
> Professor, Director for Center
> For Human-Animal Bond

Date :

Note anything unusual or outstanding about your day.

Do you want to set a dream intention? Or ask a question?

Main symbols and theme of your dream :

How did you feel when you woke from your dream?

Your interpretation :

Insights gleaned :

Action to be taken :

Give Your Dream a Title :

"Dreams are rudiments of the great state to come. We dream what is about to happen to us"
~ PHILIP JAMES BAILEY,
ENGLISH POET, AUTHOR OF FESTUS

Date : _____

Note anything unusual or outstanding about your day.

_____
_____
_____

Do you want to set a dream intention? Or ask a question?

_____
_____
_____

Main symbols and theme of your dream :

_____
_____
_____

How did you feel when you woke from your dream?

_____

Your interpretation :

_____
_____
_____

Insights gleaned :

_____
_____
_____

Action to be taken :

_____
_____

Give Your Dream a Title :

"Depending on definitions,. we spend 5 - 15 years of our lives dreaming. That's 10 years for those of us who live a long time! There must be something going on here."
~ ERNEST HARTMAN, M.D., DREAMS AND NIGHTMARES

Date : _____

Note anything unusual or outstanding about your day.

Do you want to set a dream intention? Or ask a question?

Main symbols and theme of your dream :

How did you feel when you woke from your dream?

Your interpretation :

Insights gleaned :

Action to be taken :

Give Your Dream a Title : _____

"If one advances confidently in the direction of his dreams, and endeavors to live the life which he has imagined, he will meet with success unexpected in common hours."

~ HENRY DAVID THOREAU,
AMERICAN AUTHOR, POET

Date :

Note anything unusual or outstanding about your day.

Do you want to set a dream intention? Or ask a question?

Main symbols and theme of your dream :

How did you feel when you woke from your dream?

Your interpretation :

Insights gleaned :

Action to be taken :

Give Your Dream a Title : _____

> "No one should negotiate their dreams. Dreams must be free to fly high. No government, no legislature, has a right to limit your dreams. You should never agree to surrender your dreams."
>
> ~ JESSE JACKSON,
> AMERICAN CIVIL RIGHTS ACTIVIST

Date :

Note anything unusual or outstanding about your day.

Do you want to set a dream intention? Or ask a question?

Main symbols and theme of your dream :

How did you feel when you woke from your dream?

Your interpretation :

Insights gleaned :

Action to be taken :

Give Your Dream a Title :

"Dream-sharing offers a unique vehicle for making emotional and creative contact with our children."
~ ALAN SIEGEL PhD & KELLY BULKELEY PhD, AUTHORS OF DREAMCATCHING

Date :

Note anything unusual or outstanding about your day.

Do you want to set a dream intention? Or ask a question?

Main symbols and theme of your dream :

How did you feel when you woke from your dream?

Your interpretation :

Insights gleaned :

Action to be taken :

Give Your Dream a Title :

> *"If we are fortunate enough to recall a dream, we are then ready, at some level, to be confronted by the information in the dream. This is true whether or not we choose to do so."*
> ~ Montague Ullman & Claire Limmer, The Variety of Dream Experience

Date : _____

Note anything unusual or outstanding about your day.

_____
_____
_____

Do you want to set a dream intention? Or ask a question?

_____
_____
_____

Main symbols and theme of your dream :

_____
_____
_____

How did you feel when you woke from your dream?

_____

Your interpretation :

_____
_____
_____

Insights gleaned :

_____
_____
_____

Action to be taken :

_____
_____

Give Your Dream a Title :

> "It was Jung who first put forward the evocative theory that we are dreaming all the time, and that it is only the distractions of waking life that leave us unaware of the fact."
> ~ DAVID FONTANA,
> AUTHOR, PROFESSOR

Date :

Note anything unusual or outstanding about your day.

Do you want to set a dream intention? Or ask a question?

Main symbols and theme of your dream :

How did you feel when you woke from your dream?

Your interpretation :

Insights gleaned :

Action to be taken :

Give Your Dream a Title :

> "It is beyond dispute that I can fly in dreams. You too. I add 'in my dreams' because my efforts, like yours have not succeeded— by a sound, a strangled sigh— in crossing the frontier that separates the two worlds, only one of which we designate, arbitrarily as 'real'"
>
> ~Colette,
> French Novelist

Date : _____

Note anything unusual or outstanding about your day.
_____
_____
_____

Do you want to set a dream intention? Or ask a question?
_____
_____
_____

Main symbols and theme of your dream :
_____
_____
_____

How did you feel when you woke from your dream?
_____

Your interpretation :
_____
_____
_____
_____

Insights gleaned :
_____
_____
_____

Action to be taken :
_____
_____

Give Your Dream a Title :

> "For the Aborigines of
> Australia, there is no clear
> division between dreaming
> and waking, between past,
> present, and future."
> ~ Brian Innes,
> The Book of Dreams

Date : _____

Note anything unusual or outstanding about your day.

Do you want to set a dream intention? Or ask a question?

Main symbols and theme of your dream :

How did you feel when you woke from your dream?

Your interpretation :

Insights gleaned :

Action to be taken :

Give Your Dream a Title :

> "A dream theater is an illusion within an illusion, and may appear to offer the dreamer an understanding of the mystery that lies behind the world of appearances."
> ~ DAVID FONTANA,
> THE SECRET LANGUAGE OF DREAMS

Date :

Note anything unusual or outstanding about your day.

Do you want to set a dream intention? Or ask a question?

Main symbols and theme of your dream :

How did you feel when you woke from your dream?

Your interpretation :

Insights gleaned :

Action to be taken :

Give Your Dream a Title :

> "In dreams, people experience for themselves every important kind of psychic phenomenon, and every level of helpful psychological and religious counsel."
> ~ EDGAR CAYCE,
> AMERICAN CLAIRVOYANT

Date : _____

Note anything unusual or outstanding about your day.

Do you want to set a dream intention? Or ask a question?

Main symbols and theme of your dream :

How did you feel when you woke from your dream?

Your interpretation :

Insights gleaned :

Action to be taken :

Give Your Dream a Title :

"All is like a dream or
a magic show."
~ Tibetan Buddhist Treatise,
14th Century

Date :

Note anything unusual or outstanding about your day.

Do you want to set a dream intention? Or ask a question?

Main symbols and theme of your dream :

How did you feel when you woke from your dream?

Your interpretation :

Insights gleaned :

Action to be taken :

Give Your Dream a Title :

"Many of our dreams are influenced by the stresses and fears of our waking lives."
~ MALCOLM GODWIN,
THE LUCID DREAMER

CHAPTER
FIVE

Dream Symbols and Their Meanings

$\mathcal{Y}$*our dreams are personal messages depicted in a language that you* will relate to, once you decode them. Sometimes the meaning will be obvious. Other times you will need to be a dream detective. But, don't worry, it's fun and this guide will help. Most people have the same or similar associations with common dream symbols. I've included some here. They may be accurate for you or, at the very least a good starting place to interpret the meaning of your dreams. Taking a little time to read through these can serve to "download" them into your subconscious and stimulate their use in your future dreams.

THE PEOPLE IN YOUR DREAMS

Friends, co-workers, family members, departed loved-ones, babies, strangers and even aliens may make nightly appearances in your dream dramas. Most dreams are personal messages to ourselves. Occasionally though, some people may have dreams about others that are meaningful to the other person in the dream. For example, a pregnant woman may dream of foods that contain certain nutrients for her gestating baby's needs during a specific period of development. And, "Mother's Intuition" continues in the dream-state *after* a child is born. A loving concern for anyone may open your dream into problem-solving mode on their behalf.

When dreaming of others, first ask yourself what the individual means to you? He or she may represent whatever you associate with him or her. Outgoing and bubbly, grouchy or judgmental, detail oriented or easygoing. If you have an intuitive sense, you may also try interpreting the dream as if it is a message for the other person and see if that fits. A word of caution, just because someone makes an appearance in your dream, you do not need to tell them about it, and often it is not a good idea to do so; best to use discretion.

Friends*: Friendly sign, warm, supportive, fun, closeness.* Whatever the friend's primary characteristics are, that's what they represent in your dream. If you are having a problem with a friend, the dream may be showing you how to resolve it. Your dream may also be telling you to be a better friend to yourself; to love and take care of you.

Family*: A blood connection or similar closeness.* Individual members can have the same meaning of friends above; they represent whatever you associate with them. Consider the nature of your personal relationship first. Your subconscious mind may be using the descriptors of your relationship as a symbol. Traditional roles may also apply such as; Father: breadwinner, protector, guidance, wisdom. Mother: nurturer, creative, comforting and soothing, organizes the home. A brother may represent a male aspect of the female dreamer, a buddy or a nuisance. A sister is likewise the female aspect of a male dreamer, also a companion or a tattletale. A grandmother or grandfather can represent wisdom, old-fashioned values and unconditional love.

Babies*: Since they are newly alive, babies represent something that you have created—conceived, gestated, given birth to or launched and are now nurturing along.* Your "baby" could be a new business, a creative project such as a painting or book; anything you've had in mind, and have manifested. Of course, if you actually have a baby or want to have one, your dream may be more literal in nature. But, even if you do have a baby in your life, your dream-baby may still represent an additional creative project, so, try both meanings on for size.

Departed Loved Ones: *Dreams of departed loved ones tend to fall into two categories.* The first is when, just as the other people in your dreams, your departed loved one represents what you associate or remember about that person. The second type is when the dreamer actually feels visited by their loved one. They may hear his or her laugh or smell a fragrance they remember such as Uncle Fred's cigar smoke, or Grandma's Chantilly cologne. These dreams can be very consoling. Many grieving dreamers feel that the dream was an actual last goodbye. Pay special attention to any words spoken in these types of dreams.

Co–workers: *Just as the other people in your dreams, co-workers can stand-in for whatever you associate with them in your waking state.* Many people report having unsettling dreams in which they are romantically involved with someone from the office (see, *Having Sex* in the **Dreams Of Actions** section, *pg 237*). Workplace associates can be very much like members of our family. The boss or authority person may feel in a way like a parent, peers as brothers or sisters, interns as children. Your subconscious mind may have picked up concerns or information and be trying to give you some helpful insights or a competitive edge.

Strangers: *It's fascinating that we can see people in our dreams and describe them in detail when we've never met them in our waking life.* Freud would say that you actually *have* seen this person in a crowd but didn't consciously commit their features to memory. The facial features may be symbolic. Ask yourself, *"Who does the dream person remind me of?"* A stranger can represent something different or unknown to you. Some people report visiting the same strangers repeatedly in their dreams. If the stranger is faceless he or she may represent the anima/animus, the male or female aspect of self. Or, the identity may be withheld for a reason. Ask yourself, *"Who would this be, if I knew who it was?"* And, see who pops into your mind.

Aliens: *Much like strangers but out of this world!* Aliens can represent helpful or destructive forces. In the language of dreams, aliens represent something very different or way-out-there to you.

Famous People: *Sports heroes, politicians, movie stars, television actors and newscasters can all make guest appearances in our nightly dramas.* As with others, they represent whatever you relate to them but with the additional status or exposure of being a public figure. If you dream of someone you admire, it may mean that you feel equal to them or on your way toward stardom or achievement in your field.

Animals in Your Dreams

Animals are frequent players in the theater of your mind and can represent where we feel subconsciously "out of control" to our animal natures. They can also represent instinct, and may be telling you to trust yours. Additionally, each creature represents the different characteristics associated with them. How you feel about the animal is part of its meaning. If you are afraid of it, perhaps it represents something you fear. If you adore it, then it may represent something you love, and so on. Start your interpretation by asking yourself what the animal means to you and what you think of when picturing that creature.

Lion: *King of the jungle, the lion is fierce, dangerous, beautiful and a wild beast.* Do you have someone who wants to be treated like a king in your life? Or do you carry yourself with the attitude of a true leader? In the language of dreams, all cats or felines can represent female power as well as our sensuous natures. Are you comfortable with yours?

Tiger: *Exotic, beautiful, regal and a predator.* Stripes can represent jail bars or military rank.

Bear: *Can be fierce but people have a soft feeling for bears probably due to children's fiction, animated depictions and toy teddy bears.* As with all animals, look to the unique characteristics for the dream meaning: hibernation, loves honey, the sweetness in life, great sense of smell. Also consider sound-a-likes—as in bare-naked.

Dog: *Man's best friend, can be symbolic for loyalty, unconditional love, and perpetual happiness.* Masculine symbol. Slang for feet, as in "my dogs are barking."

Cat: *Independent, self-sufficient, graceful, finicky and conditional* *love.* Feminine symbol. Subconscious sensual nature. Sleek as in cat suit, swift like a cat burglar.

Giraffe: *Obviously has a higher perspective on things.* Your dream may be suggesting that you take the high road or get a better look at the situation.

Elephant: *Enormous, something huge is happening.* Can be taught or trained but can't be ignored.

Squirrel: *Known for storing food away for the winter.* This may be a sign that it's time to stock up on essentials or tuck away some emotional reinforcement to prepare for being with a cold or difficult person.

Bugs: *What's bugging, bothering you?* Something may be irritating or annoying you. Figure out the cause and take steps to eliminate or change it.

Spiders: *Though the web is beautiful, it traps its prey and represents manipulation.* Ask yourself, *"Am I trying to overly influence someone?"* Or, *"Am I feeling pushed into something?"*

Unicorn/Pegasus/Mermaid: *This includes fantasy animals and mythical creatures.* These can remind us to play, to be whimsical or childlike in our approach to life. A suggestion to believe in some magic or a warning that your thinking is overly magical and needs an adjustment in a particular matter.

Dreams of Places

Settings in dreams can be very helpful in understanding their meaning. Additionally, since "anything goes" in dreams, the setting may change in illogical ways. That is a very significant clue to the message. Ask yourself how you feel about the location; is it familiar? Safe? The following is a brief list of common places in dreams.

Your Home: *Your current home can be a symbol for your body since we think of the body as the home of our mind, and spirit.* The kitchen represents your nutrition and digestion; the bathroom, elimination and cleansing; bedrooms are sexual activity, sleep and rest; the stairs are the spine; the attic is the brain, mind or higher-self; and the basement is your subconscious mind. If you discover rooms and items that don't exist in your actual home, your subconscious mind wants you to know that you have new parts of yourself to discover and explore. Perhaps a new talent or interest will surface and bring you great pleasure.

Childhood Home*: Our childhood home or homes are revisited frequently in dreams.* This often indicates that the dreamer is dealing in the present with something that began in our past. What happened there? What feelings do you have about that home?

Unrecognized Home*: How do you feel about this dream home?* Look closely at the outstanding features. What do they mean to you?

Store or Mall*: Opportunity, you can have anything you want, what is your choice?* Time to make a new selection?

Church*: Whether it is a church, a temple, a synagogue or other holy or sacred place, the dream will offer spiritual sustenance and deep insights.* Also, it can be the recognition of a conflict of faith in the mind of the dreamer. The heart of every faith is loving-kindness. That's a great place to start. Ask yourself, "How can I be more compassionate, loving or empathetic?"

School*: In the classic version, you are back at school.* There is a test to take and you haven't studied, maybe you can't find your classroom, or don't remember your locker combination. You feel panicked as if the outcome will not be a good one. In our adult life, this dream comes when we feel that we are not prepared for something that could judge us harshly. Ask yourself, *"What can I do now to be ready to give or do my best when called upon?"* A second meaning is that the dream will educate you in a valuable way. Important advice is being offered. Ask Yourself, *"What can I learn and how can I grow from the message of this dream?"*

Outdoors*: A forest or jungle denotes the vast unconscious mind.* What was previously unknown to you may now become known through this dream. Are you in harmony with nature? Do you need to take the "natural approach"? Perhaps your subconscious mind is suggesting that you spend more time in nature.

Dreams of Things

Items are significant in our dreams, especially when seen or used out of context to our waking life.

Hat: The roles you are playing "He's wearing a lot of hats." Also, protection from rain, sun, or cold. Wearing a hat in your dream may mean that you want to keep your thoughts to yourself. The type of hat is meaningful as well. What role are you playing and what hat are you wearing?

Bat*: Could be your turn at bat, great opportunity.* Swing hard and *"go for it!"*

Jewels*: Something of great value.* A promise of fidelity, a little something to make you stand out in a crowd. Real or costume? Also, slang for a male's sexual organs as in "the family jewels." Jewels, money and precious metals can also be symbolic of a love offering. Or literally, the concept of "love".

Books*: Refers to something new to learn.* The dream holds a lesson, same with dreams of school, a school bus, and teachers. This dream may be a suggestion that the dreamer would benefit by embarking on a new area of study. Ancient wisdom can be revealed, how old is the book?

Scissors*: Along with knives, swords and anything that cuts—can represent a need to remove something from your life or let go.* If used as a weapon, whom are you trying to get through to?

Clock*: A watch, an hourglass, a calendar—any time keeping device—can indicate the timing of something in your life.* Advice from your dream muse may be to slow-down or speed-up something. Are you concerned about missing a deadline? Is your biological clock ticking? They say, "timing is everything", and it is, except when "location is everything!" Ask yourself what you need to time or plan just right.

Telephone*: Communication, who do you need to get in-touch with?* Are you stalling? Your subconscious mind or dream source may be trying to communicate something important. Ask yourself, "What do I need to know?"

Wheelbarrow: *Carries materials, 3-wheel balance used in the garden, what seeds are you planting now.* Used in building and construction, what do you want to create in your life? Carrying a heavy load or burden? What is in the wheelbarrow?

Dreams of Vehicles

All vehicles can represent—in addition to the obvious literal item—your body; since we think of the body as the vehicle of the mind and spirit. They can indicate the dreamer's life-path or purpose and the direction they are taking for better or worse. Vehicles take us from where we are to where we're going. We say that an actor's first big movie was their vehicle to fame. How are you getting where you are going?

Airplane: *Planes and jets allow high-speed air travel.* They indicate that the dreamer is moving fast and high on their life path. A private jet could show success, prestige and wealth. Military planes indicate conflict, battling with yourself or others. Helicopters have the added ability to hover in place; are you putting something on hold? In the language of dreams, air represents our thoughts. Land represents what we know for sure or our consciousness while water represents the unconscious mind and what's below the surface. Therefore, anything in the air symbolizes what dominates our thoughts.

Automobile: *Very often associated with the body.* Is yours sleek and sporty or an old clunker? Auto dreams often contain health advice. Look at the tires as your feet, the engine your heart, headlights your eyes and so forth. If you are driving the car you are in control, making your own decisions for your life. If no one is driving your life may be out of control. If someone else is driving ask yourself, "Who have I given my power over to?" Many people dream they can't reach the brakes or the steering wheel which means life is surely out-of-control. What's the cause? Addiction? Procrastination? Whatever it is, it may be time to slow down, make better choices and take back control of your life.

Bicycle: *Balance is required to ride this vehicle and thus it is associated with a need for balance in the life of the dreamer.* Ask yourself, "Where is balance needed?" Work? Home life? Friends and family? Fast food vs. organic and home made? Also, a simple form of transportation, and a great form of exercise. Is there a need to simplify how you are moving through your life? Have you been meaning to get more exercise? Now is the time.

Motorcycle*: Read bicycle above but add the speed and noise that a motor adds.* You may be affected by a need for balance even faster or sooner. Motorcycles are also associated with being a free spirit, being part of a riding group or gang, a sense of antiestablishment philosophy. Yet, they also get good gas mileage and can get past a traffic-jam with ease. This may be a subconscious suggestion to take more leisure time, or to negotiate your way out of a jam with ease by keeping things simple.

Elevator*: In the language of dreams riding up in an elevator indicates that you are rising in status, a new title, financial gain and the like.* Moving on up! Moving down means the opposite, losing a job, losing money in the stock market, or losing face in a social situation. If the elevator moves horizontally there is no upward motion at this time. If it launches into space hold on, you're about to be a super star!

Train*: A train can only move forward or backwards along a track.* No freedom of movement, rigid. One-track mind. There is a romance about this method of transportation though, a feeling of slower times and old-fashioned manners. A subway train is different of course. Since it is underground your dream may reflect a subconscious issue or desire.

Dreams of Action

Actions are telling symbols in the language of dreams, what are you up to?

Running*: Most common in nightmares where you are being pursued.* What is gaining on you? An addiction? A deadline? An unreasonable boss or partner? If you are just running along, where are you in a hurry to? What is waiting for you there? Could be a suggestion to take up jogging!

Shooting*: Are you trying to hit a target?* What would be the bull's-eye in your life? Are you defending yourself? Against what or whom? A bow and arrow requires skill, is there a new skill you could learn that would benefit you now? If you shoot as a hobby, your gun may represent recreation. Guns, however, are also psychologically associated with male aggression; bullets with anger that wounds and penetrates. This could be a harsh judgment or criticism that stings; are you giving or receiving?

Leaping: *What are you avoiding by leaping over it.* Is your leap graceful as a ballerina or a deer? You may be jumping ahead of your competitors.

Swimming: *Many people report having fabulous swimming dreams.* Next to flying, swimming dreams are most often experienced as very pleasant. What are you swimming in? Mud? A pool? The Ocean? Each has its own meaning but swimming is generally associated with being immersed in your emotions. Swimming in mud then, you're not clear about how you feel. A pool, your emotions are contained. The ocean, you are unlimited and may also be delving into the great unconscious as well, since one theory is that all life came from the water. Many ascribe a spiritual feeling with swimming dreams. Some people report being able to breathe underwater which becomes a fabulous surprise. This can indicate comfort with feelings and emotions as opposed to feeling over your head or overwhelmed. Take note of the condition of the water. Is it calm or turbulent? Could be an indication of how your dream source perceives your emotional well-being.

Falling: *Almost everyone has had a version of this dream.* It can be related to the feeling of falling asleep, that final moment between states of consciousness. Falling dreams can be an affect of brain chemistry where you wake with a start after the "fall." But, falling dreams are also symbolically associated with a sense that you do not have a firm foundation at this time. You may not know where you stand in a relationship or situation. Falling in love is a sense that you are not in control of your emotions, love found you, but it's probably a good thing.

Flying/Floating: *Many fly on their own, arms outstretched, and love the feeling of freedom they experience.* Your flying dream may indicate the desire to rise above a situation to gain perspective. You may just need a night off, away from the "gravity" of your daily concerns. Many connect a deeply spiritual feeling with flying dreams. In the language of dreams flying upward is considered a good omen, while headed downward can mean that the dreamer perceives trouble such as losing one's job, a relationship ending, or fear of a health issue. Ask yourself, "What changes can I make to be more secure?"

Having Sex*: In the language of dreams, sex is most often a metaphor for merging with the qualities and characteristics of the partner in the dream.* How would you describe him or her? In what ways would you like to be more like him or her? Who are you "in bed with" (as in, "on the same team as")? Dream sex can also be a safe place where unconscious fantasies are played out. Both men and women can experience orgasms in their sleep, which I consider a fabulous bonus. If you have been sexually active and have become celibate for any reason, you may have sexual dreams to compensate. Much as those on a diet will dream about eating the foods they are denying themselves.

Peeing and Pooping*: If you dream you "need to go", rule out the obvious and get yourself to the bathroom.* On the other hand, when the dream is symbolic, it can mean that it is time to release something that you no longer find a benefit. This could be a partner, a job that is no longer satisfying, or an outdated way of thinking. Many people who had troubled or abusive childhoods have these types of dreams when they have been through therapy and are ready to release the victim label. Peeing is also associated with anger as in being "pissed off". Pooping can be associated with apathy as in, "I don't give a crap." The search for a suitable toilet is a common recurring dream theme. Ask yourself, "What do I need to let go of? What am I finished with? What should I release and clean up?"

Suggested Reading

If I could only have two books on dreams, (that would be a nightmare!) I would choose the following titles. One is more historic and perhaps psychological especially in the associations of dream symbols. The other is more spiritual. Looking up symbols in both gives a well-rounded beginning to uncovering your own dream symbol meanings.

Lewis, James R. — *The Dream Encyclopedia* © 1995 Visible Press

Bethards, Betty — *The Dream Book: Symbols for Self-Understanding* © 1983 Inner Light Foundation

Many of the most wonderful dream books are out of print, but thanks to the internet you are likely to find a copy. I like *Amazon.com* and *AbeBooks.com*, but there are other good resources as well.

I recommend any titles in or out of print that you can find by the following authors:

Jeremy Taylor, Patricia Garfield, Ann Faraday, Gayle Delaney, Montague Ullman & Nan Zimmerman (and of course the books he authored alone or with other authors), Carl Jung, Judith Orloff, Deirdre Barrett, Carlos Castaneda, Manly P. Hall, David Fontana, Robert L. Van de Castle, Stephen LaBerge, Charles McPhee and Edgar Cayce.

Compare, contrast, and see what methods feel right to you.

And for the related topics of sleep and the brain:

Eric Maisel, PhD — *Sleep Thinking* ©2000 Adams Media Corporation

William C. Dement MD, PhD — *The Promise of Sleep* ©1999 Dell Publishing

Allan J. Hobson, MD — *The Dreaming Brain* ©1988 Basic Books

Conclusion

"I have dreamed in my life, dreams that have stayed with me ever after, and changed my ideas; they have gone through and through me, like wine through water, and altered the colour of my mind."
~ Emily Bronte,
English Novelist and Poet

Dear Dreamer,

It is my fondest desire that this journal has been a wonderful experience for you, and I hope that you keep recording your dreams and living your best life as a result.

I'd love to hear from you. Tell me what you liked or didn't. What would you change or add. If we use your idea, I'll send you a gift of a new journal and add your name to the credits.

Without my dreams and visions, it would be terribly hard to negotiate and understand this world. My nightly dreams are my reset button! They bring me back to my center, to the beautiful truth of creation; to the process of living each day in loving kindness and compassion for all. I wake each day grateful for a new beginning, enhanced, resilient, heart open just a bit more, eyes wide open, not an ostrich with head in the sand, or a monkey hands over eyes, but perhaps a bit more courageous to venture out and give my gifts in whatever way possible to the world I encounter. I wish all this or whatever you wish for you—dreams can pave the way.

All my best wishes to you and yours,

~ *Cynthia*

"…the dreamer and his dream are the same…the powers personified in a dream are those that move the world."
~ Joseph Campbell,
American Mythologist, Philosopher, Lecturer

Made in the USA
San Bernardino, CA
25 January 2013